From Broadway To Piccadilly.

Show Stoppers.

Wise Publications.
London/New York/Sydney

Exclusive distributors:
Music Sales Limited,
8/9 Frith Street,
London W1V 5TZ,
England.

Music Sales Pty Limited,
120 Rothschild Avenue,
Rosebery, NSW 2018,
Australia.

This book © Copyright 1989 by
Wise Publications.
UK ISBN 0.7119.1424.9
Order No. AM70194

Designed by Pearce Marchbank Studio.
Compiled by Peter Evans.

Music Sales' complete catalogue lists thousands of
titles and is free from your local music shop, or direct from
Music Sales Limited. Please send £1 in stamps for postage to
Music Sales Limited, 8/9 Frith Street, London W1V 5TZ.

Printed in the United Kingdom by
The Camelot Press Limited, Southampton, Hampshire.

I Whistle A Happy Tune

Words by Oscar Hammerstein II
Music by Richard Rodgers

Whis-tle A Hap-py Tune And no one ev-er knows I'm a - fraid

The re-sult of this de - cep-tion is ver-y strange to tell For

when I fool the peo-ple I fear, I fool my-self as well! I Whis-tle A Hap-py

Tune And ev-'ry sin-gle time The hap-pi-ness in the tune con-

vin-ces me that I'm not a-fraid.

Make be-lieve you're brave And the

trick will take you far. You may be as brave as you make be-lieve you are.

Whistle

You may be as brave

as you make be-lieve you are.

It Ain't Necessarily So

Music by George Gershwin
Words by Ira Gershwin

8

A Fellow Needs A Girl

Words by Oscar Hammerstein II
Music by Richard Rodgers

All I Ask Of You

Music by Andrew Lloyd Webber
Lyrics by Charles Hart

here, with you, be-side you, to guard you and to guide you.

CHRISTINE

Say you love me ev-ery wak-ing mo-ment, turn my head with talk of summer-time.— Say you need me with you now and al-ways; pro-mise me that all you say is true, that's all I ask of

15

I'll Know

Words & Music by Frank Loesser

Standing On The Corner

Words & Music by Frank Loesser

If I Were A Bell

Words & Music by Frank Loesser

The Wells Fargo Wagon

Words & Music by Meredith Willson

Wells Far-go Wag-on is a - com - in' down the street, I wish, I wish I knew what it could
Wells Far-go Wag-on is a - com - in' down the street, I wish I knew what he was com-in'

be. ____ I got a box of ma-ple su-gar on my birth-day. ____ In
for. ____ I got some sal-mon from Se-at-tle last Sep-tem-ber. ____ And

March I got a grey mack-i-naw. And once I got some grape-fruit from
I ex-pect a new rock-in' chair. I hope I get my rais-ins from

Tam-pa. ____ Mont-gom-'ry Ward sent me a bath-tub and a cross-cut saw. O-ho, the
Fres-no. ____ The D. A. R. have sent a can-non for the court-house square. O-ho, the

Starlight Express

Music by Andrew Lloyd Webber
Lyrics by Richard Stilgoe

Star - light Ex - press, _____ are you real? Yes _____ or

no? Star - light Ex - press, _____ an - swer me "yes." _____ I

don't want you _____ to go. _____

Anywhere I Wander

Words & Music by Frank Loesser

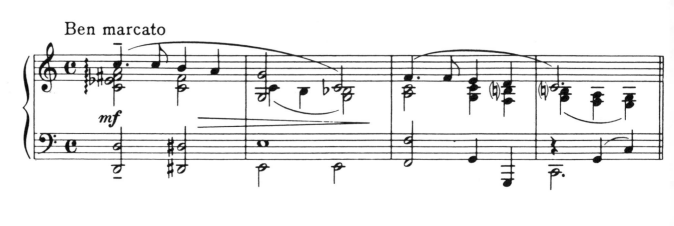

Refrain
Ben marcato

Anywhere I wander, Anywhere I roam Till I'm in the arms of my darling again My heart will find no home. Anywhere I wander, Anywhere I roam.

2. Her / His roam.
3. Her / His

My Favourite Things

Words by Oscar Hammerstein II
Music by Richard Rodgers

Rain-drops on ros-es and whisk-ers on kit-tens, Bright cop-per

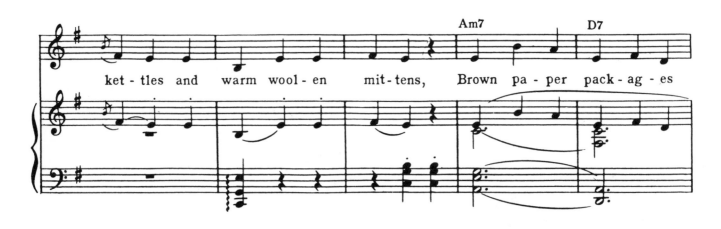

ket-tles and warm wool-en mit-tens, Brown pa-per pack-ag-es

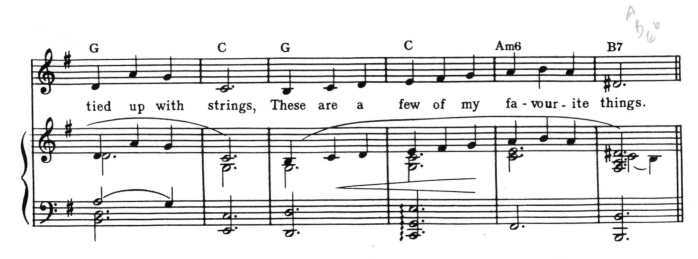

tied up with strings, These are a few of my fa-vour-ite things.

When I'm feel-ing sad,_____ I
sim-ply re-mem-ber my fa-vour-ite things and
then I don't feel so bad._____

The Music Of The Night

Music by Andrew Lloyd Webber
Lyrics by Charles Hart   Additional Lyric by Richard Stilgoe

Andante

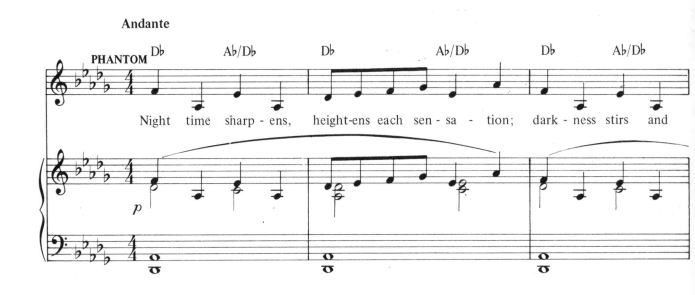

Night time sharp-ens, height-ens each sen-sa - tion; dark-ness stirs and

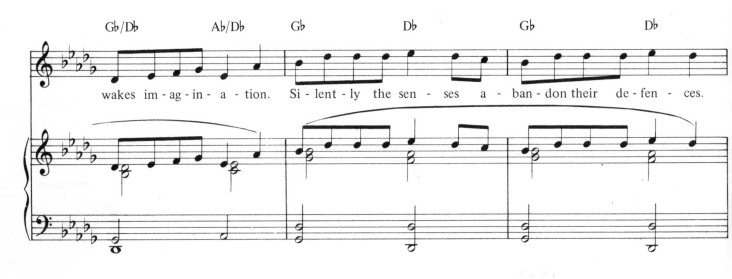

wakes im-ag-in-a-tion. Si - lent-ly the sen - ses a - ban-don their de-fen - ces.

Slow-ly, gent-ly,

night un - furls its splen - dour; grasp it, sense it, trem - u - lous and ten - der.

Turn your face a - way from the gar-ish light of day, turn your thoughts a-way from cold, un - feel-ing

light and lis-ten to the mu-sic of the night. Close your eyes and sur-ren-der to your

dark - est dreams! Purge your thoughts of the life you knew be - fore! Close your

eyes let your spi-rit start to soar and you'll live as you've nev-er lived be - fore.

Soft - ly, deft - ly, mu-sic shall ca-ress you. Hear it, feel it,

se - cret-ly po-ssess you. O - pen up your mind. let your fan-ta-sies un-wind in this

dark-ness which you know you can-not fight, the dark-ness of the mu-sic of the

night. Let your mind start a jour-ney through a strange, new world; leave all

thoughts of the world you knew be - fore. Let your soul take you where you long to

be! On - ly then can you be - long to me.

Float-ing, fall - ing, sweet in-tox-i-ca-tion. Touch me, trust me, sa-vour each sen-sa - tion.

There Is Nothin' Like A Dame

Words by Oscar Hammerstein II
Music by Richard Rodgers

G   D7

pack-ag-es from home, We get mov-ies, we get shows, We get speech-es from our
lone-ly and we long For the fair and gen-tle sex, We would like to feel the

                                       G

skip-per And ad - vice from Tok - yo Rose, We get let - ters doused with per-fume, We get
feel-ing of some arms a - round our necks. We feel hun-gry as the wolf felt When he

                     Am7   A7(b5)   D7   G

diz-zy from the smell! What don't we get? You know darn well!
met Red Rid - ing Hood. What don't we feel? We don't feel good!

marcato

B7 *Recit. (ad lib.)*   E7+   A7(b5)   D9(6)

We got nothin' to put on a clean white suit for.   We got nothin' to look masculine and __ cute for!
Lots of things in life are beautiful, but broth-er,   There is one particular thing that is nothin'
                                           whatsoever in any way, shape or form like any-oth-er.

pp

There is noth-in' like a dame, _____ Noth-in' in the world, _____ There is noth-in' you can name That is an-y-thin' like a dame!

We feel

dame!

There are no

Sixteen Going On Seventeen

Words by Oscar Hammerstein II
Music by Richard Rodgers

1. You are six- teen, go- ing on sev- en- teen,
2. I am six- teen, go- ing on sev- en- teen,

Ba- by it's time to think! Bet- ter be- ware, be can- ny and care- ful,
I know that I'm na- ive. Fel- lows I meet may tell me I'm sweet and

Ba- by you're on the brink! You are six- teen, go- ing on sev- en- teen,
will- ing- ly I'll be- lieve. I am six- teen, go- ing on sev- en- teen,

Fel- lows will fall in line. Ea- ger young lads and rou- e's and cads will
In- no- cent as a rose. Bach- e- lor dan- dies, drink- ers of bran- dies,

No Other Love

Words by Oscar Hammerstein II
Music by Richard Rodgers

Lida Rose

Words & Music by Meredith Willson

57

I Believe In You

Words & Music by Frank Loesser

Can't Help Lovin' Dat Man

Music by Jerome Kern
Words by Oscar Hammerstein II

One

Music by Marvin Hamlisch
Words by Edward Kleban

I Enjoy Being A Girl

Words by Oscar Hammer'stein II
Music by Richard Rodgers

I just lap it up like hon - ey____ I En - joy Be -

- ing A Girl! ____ I flip when a fel - low sends me

flow - ers,____ I drool o - ver dress - es made of lace,____

____ I talk on the tel - e - phone for ho - urs____ With a

pound and a half of cream up - on my face! ____ I'm strict - ly a

C7
fe - male fe - male And my fu - ture I hope will
F D7 Gm
be In the home of a brave and free male
G9 F F6 Gm B♭m
Who'll en - joy be - ing a guy hav - ing a
f
F F7 F6 C13 F
girl like me.
f
Pedal
D7-5 C7 F
When me.
f
sf
Pedal

I Ain't Down Yet

Words & Music by Meredith Willson

If I Loved You

Words by Oscar Hammerstein II
Music by Richard Rodgers

Somebody, Somewhere

Words & Music by Frank Loesser

Company

Words & Music by Stephen Sondheim

I've Never Been In Love Before

Words & Music by Frank Loesser

Ev'rybody's Got A Home But Me

Words by Richard Rodgers
Words by Oscar Hammerstein II

Slowly with warm expression

83

bod - y's Got A Home But Me._____ I am
bod - y's Got A Home But Me._____ I am

free and I'm hap - py to be free,_____ To be
free and I'm hap - py to be free,_____ To be

free in the way I want to be._____ But
free in the way I want to be._____ But

once in a while when the road is kind - a dark And the
once in a while when I'm talk - in' to my - self And the

85

Whatever Lola Wants (Lola Gets)

Words & Music by Richard Adler & Jerry Ross

Gary, Indiana

Words & Music by Meredith Willson

an - a, that's the town that knew me when. If you'd like to have a log-i-cal ex-pla - na - tion how I hap-pened on this el-e-gant syn - co - pa - tion, — I will say with-out a mo-ment of hes-i - ta-tion, — There is

How To Succeed In Business Without Really Trying

Words & Music by Frank Loesser

They Didn't Believe Me

Music by Jerome Kern
Words by Herbert Reynolds

I'm A Brass Band

Words by Dorothy Fields
Music by Cy Coleman

cla - ri - net. I'm the Phil - a -

del - phia Or - ches - tra, I'm the Mo - dern Jazz Quar - tet.

I'm Ja - scha Hei - fetz al - so Ho - ro - witz,
I'm the band from Ma - cy's big pa - rade. A

wild Count Ba - sie blast. I'm the bells of Saint

Pe - ter's in Rome _____ I'm tis-sue pa-per on a comb. _____

And all _____ kinds of mu - sic _____

_____ is pour - ing out of me 'cause

some - bo - dy loves me _____ at last! _____ Now,

Last! _____

Do You Hear The People Sing?

Music by Claude-Michel Schonberg
Lyrics by Herbert Kretzmer
Original Text by Alain Boublil & Jean-Marc Natel

Do you hear the peo - ple sing? Sing-ing the
song of an - gry men? It is the mu - sic of a peo - ple Who will
not be slaves a - gain! When the bea - ting of your heart Ech - oes the
bea - ting of the drums There is a life a - bout to start When to-mor-row comes! Will you

join in our cru-sade? Who will be strong and stand with me? Be-
give all you can give So that our ban-ner may ad-vance? Some will

-yond the bar-ri-cade Is there a world you ___ long to see? Then
fall, and some will live. Will you stand up and ___ take your chance? The

join in the fight That will give you the right to be free!
blood of the mar-tyrs Will wa-ter the mea-dows of France!

Do you

hear the peo-ple sing? Sing-ing the song of an-gry men? It is the

102

The Rhythm Of Life

Words by Dorothy Fields
Music by Cy Coleman

Great Day

Words by William Rose & Edward Eliscu
Music by Vincent Youmans

Ol' Man River

Music by Jerome Kern
Words by Oscar Hammerstein II

Slowly

Ol' man riv-er, dat ol' man riv-er, He must know sump-in', but don't say noth-in', He

jus' keeps roll-in', He keeps on roll-in' a- long. _____ He

don't plant 'ta-ters, he don't plant cot-ton, An' dem dat plants 'em is soon for-got-ten, But

Master Of The House

Music by Claude-Schonberg   Lyric by Herbert Kretzmer
Original Text by Alain Boublil & Jean-Marc Natel

Dm9 ... Am9

Sel-dom do you see ____
Here the goose is cooked ____

Hon-est men like me
Here the fat is fried

A
And

B7 ... E ... F♯m ... E7

gent of good in - tent
no-thing's ov - er - looked

Who's con - tent to be
Till I'm sa - tis - fied...

A

mf

Ma -ster of the House
Food be-yond com-pare

Do-ling out the charm
Food be-yond be- lief

Rea-dy with a hand-shake And an o - pen palm
Mix it in a min - cer And pre-tend it's beef.

B7

Tells a sauc-y tale
Kid-ney of a horse

Makes a lit - tle stir
Li - ver of a cat

Cust-om-ers ap-pre - ci-ate a bon - vi-veur!
Fill - ing up the sau - sa - ges With this and that!

Glad to do my friends a fa - vour ____ Does-n't cost me to be nice but
Re - si -dents are more than wel - come ____ Bri - dal suite is oc - cu - pied! ____

no -thing gets you no - thing Ev - 'ry-thing has got a lit - tle price! ____
Rea -son - a - ble charg - es Plus ___ some lit - tle ex - tra on the side! ____

Mas - ter of the House Keep-er of the zoo Rea-dy to re - lieve them of a
Charge 'em for the lice Ex - tra for the mice Two per-cent for look-ing in the

sou, or two. Wa-ter -ing the wine Ma-king up the weight Pick-ing up their knick-knacks When they
mir - ror twice! Here a lit - tle slice There a lit- tle cut Three percent for sleep - ing with the

120

There's Gotta Be Something Better Than This

Words by Dorothy Fields
Music by Cy Coleman

Thumbelina

Words & Music by Frank Loesser